On the Move: Animal Migration

Three Informational Texts

by Thea Feldman

Table of Contents

Informational Texts

What is an informational text?

An informational text is a nonfiction text that presents information in an accurate and organized way. It is often about a single subject such as animal behavior, an event or time period in history, or a scientific discovery. It may be about any topic, such as an annual event or a hobby. The research report that you write for a school assignment is an informational text. So is an article you read in your favorite fashion magazine or on a Web site. A newspaper account of a local election and a history book chapter on a famous battle are additional examples of informational texts.

What is the purpose of informational texts?

Informational texts have one main purpose: to inform. The best informational writing does this in a way that keeps readers' attention. It pulls readers in and makes them want to keep reading and to know more about the topic.

How do you read an informational text?

When you read informational texts, look for facts and the details that support them. Read critically to make sure conclusions make sense. If there is more than one way to look at an event or situation, make sure it is given. Ask yourself: *Did I learn something new from this text? Do I want to know more about it? Can I draw my own conclusions from what I have read?*

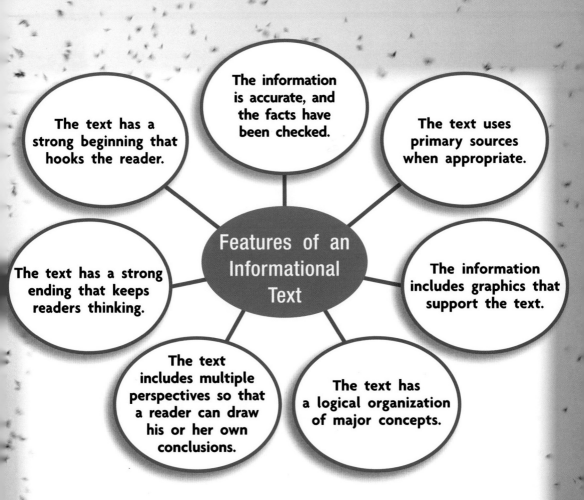

The text has a strong beginning that hooks the reader.

The information is accurate, and the facts have been checked.

The text uses primary sources when appropriate.

Features of an Informational Text

The text has a strong ending that keeps readers thinking.

The information includes graphics that support the text.

The text includes multiple perspectives so that a reader can draw his or her own conclusions.

The text has a logical organization of major concepts.

Who writes informational texts?

Writers who know their topic well write good informational text. They do this by becoming mini-experts on the subject they are writing about. They make sure that they support the information in their work with historical facts, scientific data, graphics like time lines and diagrams, and expert evidence. They provide more than one person's point of view. They use primary sources, or first-hand information, like journals and photographs.

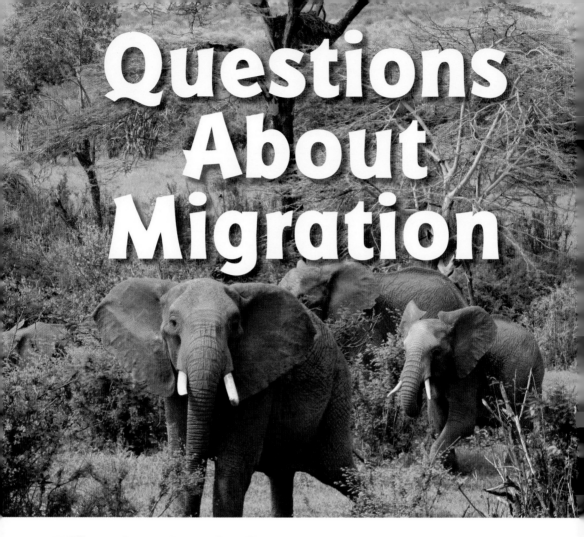

Questions About Migration

What is migration?
Migration is when animals move from one place
to another.

Do all animals migrate?
Not all animals migrate. But some kinds of mammals,
fish, birds, and insects do.

Where do animals migrate?
Animals migrate on land, in the water, or in the sky.
They walk, swim, or fly to get where they need to go.

Why do animals migrate?

Some animals are looking for food and water. That is why African elephants migrate. Some animals are looking for safe places to have babies or lay eggs. That is why sea turtles migrate. Some animals are looking for warm weather. That is why bluebirds fly south when the weather turns cold.

When do animals migrate?

Most animals that migrate do so every year at the same time. They go to the same place year after year, too. They stay for a while. Then they go back to their homes. They stay until it is time to migrate again.

Tools Writers Use

A Strong Lead

A strong lead, or opening section, grabs or "hooks" readers. A strong lead makes readers want to keep reading. The lead tells you something important about the subject and hints at what you may learn. Writers use two types of leads. A direct lead tells who or what the piece is about and why the subject is important. An indirect lead may quote someone, ask a question, describe a setting, or tell a story about the subject.

About 1.5 million gnus (a type of antelope) and a half million zebras migrate each year in Africa.

Migrating Animals on Land

Can you imagine two million gnus (NOOS) and zebras taking a very, very long walk? Think about all those animals together. And the noise from their hooves! Every fall that is exactly what gnus and zebras do. They leave their home in Kenya, Africa, and migrate south. They go away for many months. In the spring they walk back north. They travel 1,800 miles in all.

There are many dangers along the way. If an animal falls, it could be trampled. Or a **predator**, such as a lion or crocodile, could attack. So why do the gnus and zebras migrate? They are looking for food and water. These animals eat grass. There is none left where they live. The ground is dry. There is no fresh water to drink.

It begins to rain in the fall. Where it rains, grass will soon grow. So the animals follow the rain. They go south to Tanzania. They walk across an area that has sweet, fresh grass and cool water.

The gnus and zebras eat and eat. Many baby gnus are born in Tanzania. They grow quickly and are ready to migrate north with the others in the spring. By the time the gnus and zebras get back to Kenya, there is new grass and water there. The animals will stay until the food is gone and the rains start again.

Circular migration of gnus and zebras in Kenya and Tanzania

Caribou migrate south of the Arctic Circle in the fall.

Far across the world, fall is also when caribou (KAIR-ih-boo) leave their homes. A caribou is a large deer. (Caribou are also known as reindeer.) The caribou of Alaska in the United States and parts of Canada spend summer near the Arctic Circle. But in the fall, the **temperature** drops. It gets very cold. A lot of snow falls. The snow covers the grass. The caribou cannot get to the grass. They must leave or they will starve and freeze to death.

During summer, caribou live **solitary** lives. But during the fall migration, up to 100,000 will travel south together. Caribou try to stay safe from wolves. They must swim through cold, strong rivers. They must be careful not to fall on the ice and break a leg.

The caribou will spend winter in forests below the Arctic Circle. In June, pregnant females will head north first. They will give birth back in the Arctic. It is warm there again with plenty to eat. And there are no wolves to threaten them or their young.

8

Caribou face dangers to make sure their babies are born in a safe place. So do the red crabs of Christmas Island, near Australia. Every November, fifty million crabs migrate to mate and lay their eggs. The crabs travel from the forest to the beach. There they mate. Then the females will release their eggs in the ocean.

Each crab is about the size of a dinner plate. They normally do not move very much or go very far. But during mating season, the crabs crawl for ten days or more. They cross roads and crawl through buildings!

In fall, the red crabs of Christmas Island migrate from the forests.

This is dangerous for the crabs. But the biggest danger comes from ants called yellow crazy ants. These ants attack crabs. They are defending their **territory**. When the ants attack, they spray acid. If the spray gets in a crab's eyes, the crab can get confused and die.

Each female crab lays up to 100,000 eggs in the sea. Then the crabs leave. The eggs hatch quickly. The baby crabs grow in the sea for a month. Then they come to shore and begin to crawl to the forest. They will finish growing there. And someday the baby crabs will migrate to the shore to have their own babies.

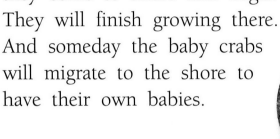

The red crabs go to the beaches to lay eggs.

Analyze the Text

- Why do gnus and zebras migrate?
- How are the zebras and caribou alike?
- The text says that the animals face many dangers as they migrate, but they do it anyway. What does this tell you about these animals?
- This informational text uses descriptive text structure. Find three examples.

Analyze the Tools Writers Use: A Strong Lead

Look at the lead in the informational article.

- Did the author use a direct lead or an indirect lead? How can you tell?
- Did the lead "hook" you as a reader? Why?
- What did you expect to learn after reading the lead?

Focus on Words: Word Origins

A word's origin is the history of that word. Many words in English come from words in other languages, especially Latin and Greek. For example, **migration** comes from Latin and means "the act of wandering or moving." *Migra* means "to move or wander" and *-ation* is "the act of doing something." Knowing the history of a word can help you understand its meaning. Make a chart like the one below. Use a dictionary to find the origin and meaning of the words from the text.

Page	Word	Origin and Meaning	Dictionary Definition
6	predator		
8	temperature		
8	solitary		
10	territory		

Migrating Animals in the Sea

C ould you go for eight months without eating? If you were a gray whale, you could. Gray whales do that every year when they migrate.

Before they migrate south, these **marine** mammals swim in the cold water near the North Pole. They get plenty to eat there. The arctic sea is filled with shrimp and tube worms. But the sea gets colder and colder as summer comes to an end. The whales have to leave before the water turns to ice.

In the fall, the first whales leave in a group. These are the pregnant females. They must travel south before they give birth. They will have their babies in the Pacific Ocean. The babies will be born in the warm waters off the coast of Baja California and other places in Mexico.

Sometimes the whales swim near the shore as they travel. When this happens people can see them. Every few minutes the whales rise up out of the water. They come up to take a breath. It is a **magnificent** sight that people enjoy year after year.

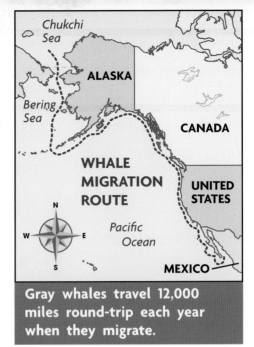

Gray whales travel 12,000 miles round-trip each year when they migrate.

The journey south takes up to three months. The whales stay south for another two to three months. Then they begin the journey home. The shrimp and tube worms they eat do not live in the southern waters. That is why they do not eat for the **duration** of their migration.

How does a gray whale survive without food? It lives off its fat, or blubber. A fully grown gray whale can weigh nearly 80,000 pounds and be more than forty-five feet long!

Tourists watch for migrating whales off the coast of California.

An animal does not need to be big to migrate in the sea, however. Baby eels no more than a **quarter** inch long migrate, too. The eels are so small they look like tiny leaves.

These eels are born in the Sargasso Sea. The Sargasso Sea is located in the Atlantic Ocean. The tiny eels float in the water for a year. When they reach the Atlantic coast of North America, they begin to grow and change. They begin to look more like eels than leaves. They are called glass eels because you can see through their bodies!

The eels keep growing for ten years. The females will be almost twice the size of the males. After ten years the eels return to the Sargasso Sea. They mate and give birth there. Then they die. Thousands of tiny baby eels begin the journey their parents took before them.

SARGASSO EEL MIGRATION ROUTE

NORTH AMERICA

Sargasso Sea

Atlantic Ocean

SOUTH AMERICA

N
W—E
S

Reread the Informational Text

Analyze the Text
- Why do pregnant whales leave the group first?
- What does a gray whale live off of during migration?
- Why were glass eels given that name?
- How are whales and glass eels different, apart from their size?
- It takes a long time for glass eels to grow up. How can you tell?

Analyze the Tools Writers Use: A Strong Lead

Look at the lead in the informational article.
- Did the author use a direct lead or an indirect lead? How can you tell?
- Did the lead "hook" you as a reader? Why?
- What did you expect to learn after reading the lead?

Focus on Words: Word Origins

Knowing the history of a word can help you understand its meaning. Make a chart like the one below. Use a dictionary to find the origin and meaning of the words from the text.

Page	Word	Origin and Meaning	Dictionary Definition
12	marine		
13	magnificent		
13	duration		
14	quarter		

Migrating Animals in the Sky

Which animal migrates the farthest distance? The world record holder is the arctic tern. This bird flies 25,000 miles round-trip! That is the flying distance from the North Pole to the South Pole. The arctic tern does this every year. It flies for most of its life.

Why does the arctic tern do this? The bird likes summer! That may sound strange for a bird that lives in the two coldest places on Earth. But the arctic tern spends the summer at the North Pole. When summer is over at the North Pole, it becomes summer at the South Pole. The arctic tern flies 12,500 miles one way so it can have a **second** summer!

Arctic tern babies are born at the North Pole. The mother and father feed the babies a lot of fish. Everyone needs to be strong to travel so far. Along the way, the birds may grab fish out of the water. They will eat while flying! They land only rarely and for a short time. It takes them about eight months to reach the South Pole. They eat a lot of fish there. When summer ends, the arctic terns **proceed** back to the North Pole.

Monarch butterflies do not like the cold, either. They cannot survive when the temperature drops below 60°F (15.5°C). That is why millions of monarch butterflies leave home every year. They meet and fly away from North America and Canada. They fly south to Mexico. While in Mexico, they rest on trees in the warm sun. In Mexico they eat and mate. In spring, the butterflies fly home. They may fly as many as 6,000 miles round-trip. But the butterflies that go south are not the ones that return north. It is their grandchildren!

Most butterflies live for about one month. But scientists, including those at the Wildlife Conservation Society, know that some monarchs live longer. The monarchs that fly south are called **migrants.** Migrants can live for up to nine months. They make the entire trip south. But they do not make the entire trip north again.

Migrants begin to fly north in spring. Only the females go. The males die in Mexico. Along the way the females lay eggs on milkweed plants. Then the females die. It is April. In a few weeks, the eggs hatch. The young become adults in a few weeks. Then they begin to fly north.

They fly until June. Then these butterflies lay their eggs. After that, these butterflies die, too. They did not live as long as their parents, the migrants.

When the new young butterflies become adults, they fly north. They will finish the trip. They are the grandchildren of the migrants. And they will be the migrants that fly south the next fall.

How do these butterflies know to fly to a place they have never seen? Some scientists think they follow the sun. Other scientists think they follow their instincts.

Scientists at the Warnell School of Forestry and Natural Resources have learned that the monarchs that travel the farthest have the largest and most narrow wings. These scientists believe that the wing size helps the butterflies carry fat deposits to fuel the journey.

Studies conducted by Dr. Zoey Katz, an insect expert in New York City, support the Warnell study. Dr. Katz says, "The wing shape of the eastern monarchs is a lot like those of other flying animals that migrate. This shape helps flying animals move through the air easily."

The author provides different ideas about how monarchs migrate. She is showing that there are different perspectives on this scientific concept.

The author includes a word-for-word quote from an expert she interviewed. This is a primary source.

Monarch Butterfly Migration Route

Vancouver, Canada: 2,440 miles to Angangueo, Mexico

St. John, North Dakota: 2,030 miles to Angangueo, Mexico

Brunswick, Maine: 2,384 miles to Angangueo, Mexico

ATLANTIC OCEAN

PACIFIC OCEAN

GULF OF MEXICO

N W E S

Angangueo, Mexico

0 500 MILES
0 800 KILOMETERS

A swarm of migrating locusts feeds on a bush in the Sahara Desert.

The author includes a graphic (above) that visually illustrates the content.

The author's ending comes back to the overall theme that some animals are on the move and that migrations happen over and over. This idea should intrigue the reader to want to learn more about this amazing behavior in the animal kingdom.

Some animals, like arctic terns and monarch butterflies, migrate every year. Other animals do this only once in a while. Some insects in Africa migrate only when too many of them are born at the same time in the same place, and there is not enough food for them all. So these insects, called locusts, take to the skies in search of food. There can be billions of hungry locusts in the air at once!

The locusts eat every plant they find and keep flying. New locusts are born and old locusts die. Then one day there is a balance of locusts and food. So, the locusts stay in one place again—until the next time they need to migrate.

Analyze the Text

- What do arctic terns eat while traveling from pole to pole?
- What happens to female monarchs after they lay their eggs?
- How are the arctic tern and the monarch butterfly alike? How are they different?
- What do the last two paragraphs tell us about migrating animals?
- The author says that monarch butterflies do not like the cold, either. She also says that, "Other animals only do this once in a while." What text structure is this?

Analyze the Tools Writers Use: A Strong Lead

Look at the lead in the informational article.

- Did the author use a direct lead or an indirect lead? How can you tell?
- What did you expect to learn after reading the lead?
- Did the lead "hook" you as a reader? Why?

Focus on Words: Word Origins

Knowing the history of a word can help you understand its meaning. Make a chart like the one below. Use a dictionary to find the origin and meaning of the words from the text.

Page	Word	Origin and Meaning	Dictionary Definition
16	second		
17	proceed		
18	migrants		

How does an author write an Informational Text?

Reread "Migrating Animals in the Sky" and think about what Thea Feldman did to write this informational text. How did she keep a narrow focus? How did she help you understand the text?

1. Decide on a Topic

Choose something you are interested in and want to know more about. Good writers enjoy researching their topics.

2. Narrow Your Focus

Thea Feldman knew she couldn't write everything there is to know about animals that migrate in the sky, so she narrowed her focus to three examples: arctic terns, monarch butterflies, and locusts.

3. Write a Question about Your Focus

Questions lead to answers, so turn your focus into a question.

4. Research Your Focus

Become the "expert" by reading articles on the Internet, books, and newspaper articles, and by interviewing people connected with your topic. For instance, Thea used research findings from the Wildlife Conservation Society and interviewed Dr. Katz. You want to show readers that you know what you are talking about.

5. Organize Your Information

Before writing an informational article, make a chart or table like the one on the next page that outlines the main points. For each main point, identify supporting details. You don't have to write full sentences. These are your notes. Remember, however, that there should be a logical progression of ideas.

6. Write Your Informational Text

As you write, develop each main point with your supporting details. Remember, you want people to enjoy reading your article as well as learn something new.

Topic: animals that migrate in the sky
Focus: arctic terns, monarch butterflies, and locusts
Question: Why and how do some flying animals migrate?

Main Point	Details
Introduction	Arctic terns migrate farther than other animals. Travel 25,000 miles round-trip.
Why arctic terns migrate	Live near North Pole. Don't like cold weather. Need to leave before ice forms.
The journey	Birds fly 12,500 miles one way. They grab fish from ocean and eat while flying. They land rarely and only for a short time. They travel for eight months to reach South Pole, where it is then summer.
Why monarch butterflies migrate	They cannot survive in cold weather.
The journey	Monarchs travel as much as 6,000 miles round-trip. "Migrants" travel from U.S. and Canada to Mexico and spend winter there. Migrants fly north, lay eggs, and die. New butterflies continue journey. They lay eggs and die, too. Grandchildren of migrants finish journey. They become the next migrants.
Why locusts migrate	Sometimes there is not enough food.
The journey	Billions fly together looking for food. Eat everything they can and keep flying. Young locusts join and old locusts die. The migration will continue until there is enough food to feed them all.

Glossary

duration   (duh-RAY-shun) the time it takes to do something (page 13)

magnificent   (mag-NIH-fih-sent) amazingly beautiful and impressive (page 13)

marine   (muh-REEN) having to do with the sea (page 12)

migrants   (MY-grunts) animals that travel from one place to live to another (page 18)

predator   (PREH-duh-ter) an animal that kills and eats other animals (page 6)

proceed   (proh-SEED) to move along in an orderly way (page 17)

quarter   (KWOR-ter) one of four parts; one-fourth (page 14)

second   (SEH-kund) another (page 16)

solitary   (SAH-lih-tair-ee) alone; not part of a group (page 8)

temperature   (TEM-puh-ruh-cher) a measured amount of hotness or coldness (page 8)

territory   (TAIR-ih-tor-ee) the area where animals find food, have their babies, and live (page 10)